April, A Month In Verse

Poetry is a fascinating use of language. With almost a million words at its command it is not surprising that these Isles have produced some of the most beautiful, moving and descriptive verse through the centuries. In this series we look at each calendar month through the eyes and minds of our most gifted poets to bring you a guide to the days within each.

This volume of Poetry is all about **April** - the fourth month of the year in our Gregorian calendar heralding Spring in earnest and of course April Showers and perhaps other unsettled weather. For our poets including Wilfred Owen, Thomas Hardy, Robert Louis Stevenson, Henry Alford, Robert Browning, Henry Van Dyke, Percy Byssche Shelley and Henry Wadsworth Longfellow the month provides a rich source for them to muse upon.   Many of the poems are also available as an audiobook from our sister company Portable Poetry. Many samples are at our youtube channel http://www.youtube.com/user/PortablePoetry?feature=mhee   The full volume can be purchased from iTunes, Amazon and other digital stores. Among the readers are Richard Mitchley and Ghizela Rowe

Index Of Poems
It Was An April morning Fresh And Clear by William Wordsworth

An April Day by Henry Wadsworth Longfellow

Elegy In April And September by Wilfred Owen

April by Sara Teasdale

Over The Land In April by Robert Louis Stevenson

April by Algernon Charles Swinburne

My April Lady by Henry Van Dyke

Rome: Building A New Street In The Ancient Quarter (April, 1887) by Thomas Hardy

An April Love by Alfred Austin

A Petition To April, Written During Sickness by Susanna Blamire

Endorsement To The Deed Of Separation In The April Of 1816 by Lord George Gordon Byron

Stanzas April 1814 by Percy Bysshe Shelley

A Letter To Dafnis April: 2d 1685 by Anne Kingsmill Finch

On A Nightingale In April by William Sharp

Spinning In April by Josephine Preston Peabody

San Francisco: April 18,1906 by Ina D Coolbirth

Here By The Brimming April Streams by Phillip Henry Savage

Hastings In April by Bessie Rayner Parkes

Love Like An April Day Beguiles by James Bland Burges

April by John Bannister Tabb

April Showers by Menella Bute Smedley

An April Gust by Elizabeth Stuart Phelps Ward

Stanzas To April And Invitation To Garibaldi by Janet Hamilton

The Soul Of April by Bliss William Carman

Under The April Moon by Bliss William Carman

April Evening, France, April 1916 by John William Streets

Sonnet To April by Henry Kirke White

April – And Dying by Anne Reeve Aldrich

Written April 18th 1796 by Matilda Betham

Written On The Day Of General Thanksgiving April 14th 1833 by Henry Alford

An April Fool by Alfred Austin

Be Ye In Love With April Tide by Clinton Scollard

April 1844 by Henry Alford

The Famous Speech-Maker Of England Or Baron (Alias Barren) Lovel's Charge At The Assizes At Exon, April 5, 1710 by Jonathan Swift

The Idler's Calendar. Twelve Sonnets For The Month. April by Wilfred Scawen Blunt

Child's Talk In April by Christina Georgina Rossetti

Home Thoughts From Abroad by Robert Browning

It Was An April morning Fresh And Clear by William Wordsworth
It was an April morning: fresh and clear
The Rivulet, delighting in its strength,
Ran with a young man's speed; and yet the voice
Of waters which the winter had supplied
Was softened down into a vernal tone.

The spirit of enjoyment and desire,
And hopes and wishes, from all living things
Went circling, like a multitude of sounds.
The budding groves seemed eager to urge on
The steps of June; as if their various hues
Were only hindrances that stood between
Them and their object: but, meanwhile, prevailed
Such an entire contentment in the air
That every naked ash, and tardy tree
Yet leafless, showed as if the countenance
With which it looked on this delightful day
Were native to the summer.--Up the brook
I roamed in the confusion of my heart,
Alive to all things and forgetting all.
At length I to a sudden turning came
In this continuous glen, where down a rock
The Stream, so ardent in its course before,
Sent forth such sallies of glad sound, that all
Which I till then had heard, appeared the voice
Of common pleasure: beast and bird, the lamb,
The shepherd's dog, the linnet and the thrush
Vied with this waterfall, and made a song,
Which, while I listened, seemed like the wild growth
Or like some natural produce of the air,
That could not cease to be. Green leaves were here;
But 'twas the foliage of the rocks--the birch,
The yew, the holly, and the bright green thorn,
With hanging islands of resplendent furze:
And, on a summit, distant a short space,
By any who should look beyond the dell,
A single mountain-cottage might be seen.
I gazed and gazed, and to myself I said,
"Our thoughts at least are ours; and this wild nook,
My EMMA, I will dedicate to thee."
----Soon did the spot become my other home,
My dwelling, and my out-of-doors abode.

And, of the Shepherds who have seen me there,
To whom I sometimes in our idle talk
Have told this fancy, two or three, perhaps,
Years after we are gone and in our graves,
When they have cause to speak of this wild place,
May call it by the name of EMMA'S DELL.

An April Day by Henry Wadsworth Longfellow
When the warm sun, that brings
Seed-time and harvest, has returned again,
'T is sweet to visit the still wood, where springs
The first flower of the plain.

I love the season well,
When forest glades are teeming with bright forms,
Nor dark and many-folded clouds foretell
The coming-on of storms.

From the earth's loosened mould
The sapling draws its sustenance, and thrives;
Though stricken to the heart with winter's cold,
The drooping tree revives.

The softly-warbled song
Comes from the pleasant woods, and colored wings
Glance quick in the bright sun, that moves along
The forest openings.

When the bright sunset fills
The silver woods with light, the green slope throws
Its shadows in the hollows of the hills,
And wide the upland glows.

And when the eve is born,
In the blue lake the sky, o'er-reaching far,
Is hollowed out and the moon dips her horn,
And twinkles many a star.

Inverted in the tide
Stand the gray rocks, and trembling shadows throw,
And the fair trees look over, side by side,
And see themselves below.

Sweet April! many a thought
Is wedded unto thee, as hearts are wed;
Nor shall they fail, till, to its autumn brought,
Life's golden fruit is shed.

Elegy In April And September by Wilfred Owen
Hush, thrush! Hush, missen-thrush, I listen
I heard the flush of footsteps through the loose leaves,
And a low whistle by the water's brim.

Still! Daffodil! Nay, hail me not so gaily,-
Your gay gold lily daunts me and deceives,
Who follow gleams more golden and more slim.

Look, brook! O run and look, O run!
The vain reeds shook? - Yet search till gray sea heaves,
And I will stray among these fields for him.

Gaze, daisy! Stare through haze and glare,
And mark the hazardous stars all dawns and eves,

For my eye withers, and his star wanes dim.

Close, rose, and droop, heliotrope,
And shudder, hope! The shattering winter blows.
Drop, heliotrope, and close, rose

Mourn, corn, and sigh, rye.
Men garner you, but youth's head lies forlorn.
Sigh, rye, and mourn, corn

Brood, wood, and muse, yews,
The ways gods use we have not understood.
Muse, yews, and brood, wood

April by Sara Teasdale
The roofs are shining from the rain.
The sparrows tritter as they fly,
And with a windy April grace
The little clouds go by.

Yet the back-yards are bare and brown
With only one unchanging tree--
I could not be so sure of Spring
Save that it sings in me.

Over The Land In April by Robert Louis Stevenson
Over the land is April,
Over my heart a rose;
Over the high, brown mountain
The sound of singing goes.
Say, love, do you hear me,
Hear my sonnets ring?
Over the high, brown mountain,
Love, do you hear me sing?

By highway, love, and byway
The snows succeed the rose.
Over the high, brown mountain
The wind of winter blows.
Say, love, do you hear me,
Hear my sonnets ring?
Over the high, brown mountain
I sound the song of spring,
I throw the flowers of spring.
Do you hear the song of spring?
Hear you the songs of spring?

Child's Talk In April by Christina Georgina Rosetti

I wish you were a pleasant wren,
And I your small accepted mate;
How we'd look down on toilsome men!
We'd rise and go to bed at eight
Or it may be not quite so late.

Then you should see the nest I'd build,
The wondrous nest for you and me;
The outside rough perhaps, but filled
With wool and down; ah, you should see
The cosy nest that it would be.

We'd have our change of hope and fear,
Small quarrels, reconcilements sweet:
I'd perch by you to chirp and cheer,
Or hop about on active feet,
And fetch you dainty bits to eat.

We'd be so happy by the day,
So safe and happy through the night,
We both should feel, and I should say,
It's all one season of delight,
And we'll make merry whilst we may,

Perhaps some day there'd be an egg
When spring had blossomed from the snow:
I'd stand triumphant on one leg;
Like chanticleer I'd almost crow
To let our little neighbours know.

Next you should sit and I would sing
Through lengthening days of sunny spring;
Till, if you wearied of the task,
I'd sit; and you should spread your wing
From bough to bough; I'd sit and bask.

Fancy the breaking of the shell,
The chirp, the chickens wet and bare,
The untried proud paternal swell;
And you with housewife-matron air
Enacting choicer bills of fare.

Fancy the embryo coats of down,
The gradual feathers soft and sleek;
Till clothed and strong from tail to crown,
With virgin warblings in their beak,
They too go forth to soar and seek.

So would it last an April through
And early summer fresh with dew,
Then should we part and live as twain:

Love-time would bring me back to you
And build our happy nest again.

April by Algernon Charles Swinburne

When the fields catch flower
And the underwood is green,
And from bower unto bower
The songs of the birds begin,
I sing with sighing between.
When I laugh and sing,
I am heavy at heart for my sin;
I am sad in the spring
For my love that I shall not win,
For a foolish thing.

This profit I have of my woe,
That I know, as I sing,
I know he will needs have it so
Who is master and king,
Who is lord of the spirit of spring.
I will serve her and will not spare
Till her pity awake
Who is good, who is pure, who is fair,
Even her for whose sake
Love hath ta'en me and slain unaware.

O my lord, O Love,
I have laid my life at thy feet;
Have thy will thereof,
Do as it please thee with it,
For what shall please thee is sweet.
I am come unto thee
To do thee service, O Love;
Yet cannot I see
Thou wilt take any pity thereof,
Any mercy on me.

But the grace I have long time sought
Comes never in sight,
If in her it abideth not,
Through thy mercy and might,
Whose heart is the world's delight.
Thou hast sworn without fail I shall die,
For my heart is set
On what hurts me, I wot not why,
But cannot forget
What I love, what I sing for and sigh.

She is worthy of praise,
For this grief of her giving is worth
All the joy of my days

That lie between death's day and birth,
All the lordship of things upon earth.
Nay, what have I said?
I would not be glad if I could;
My dream and my dread
Are of her, and for her sake I would
That my life were fled.

Lo, sweet, if I durst not pray to you,
Then were I dead;
If I sang not a little to say to you,
(Could it be said)
O my love, how my heart would be fed;
Ah sweet who hast hold of my heart,
For thy love's sake I live,
Do but tell me, ere either depart,
What a lover may give
For a woman so fair as thou art.
The lovers that disbelieve,
False rumours shall grieve
And evil-speaking shall part.

My April Lady by Henry Van Dyke

When down the stair at morning
The sunbeams round her float,
Sweet rivulets of laughter
Are bubbling in her throat;
The gladness of her greeting
Is gold without alloy;
And in the morning sunlight
I think her name is Joy.

When in the evening twilight
The quiet book-room lies,
We read the sad old ballads,
While from her hidden eyes
The tears are falling, falling,
That give her heart relief;
And in the evening twilight,
I think her name is Grief.

My little April lady,
Of sunshine and of showers,
She weaves the old spring magic,
And breaks my heart in flowers!
But when her moods are ended,
She nestles like a dove;
Then, by the pain and rapture,
I know her name is Love.

Rome: Building A New Street In The Ancient Quarter (April, 1887) by Thomas Hardy
These numbered cliffs and gnarls of masonry
Outskeleton Time's central city, Rome;
Whereof each arch, entablature, and dome
Lies bare in all its gaunt anatomy.

And cracking frieze and rotten metope
Express, as though they were an open tome
Top-lined with caustic monitory gnome;
"Dunces, Learn here to spell Humanity!"

And yet within these ruins' very shade
The singing workmen shape and set and join
Their frail new mansion's stuccoed cove and quoin
With no apparent sense that years abrade,
Though each rent wall their feeble works invade
Once shamed all such in power of pier and groin.

An April Love by Alfred Austin
Nay, be not June, nor yet December, dear,
But April always, as I find thee now:
A constant freshness unto me be thou,
And not the ripeness that must soon be sere.
Why should I be Time's dupe, and wish more near
The sobering harvest of thy vernal vow?
I am content, so still across thy brow
Returning smile chase transitory tear.
Then scatter thy April heart in sunny showers;
I crave nor Summer drouth nor Winter sleet:
As Spring be fickle, so thou be as sweet;
With half-kept promise tantalise the hours;
And let Love's frolic hands and woodland feet
Fill high the lap of Life with wilding flowers.

A Petition To April, Written During Sickness by Susanna Blamire
Sweet April! month of all the year
That loves to shed the dewy tear,
And with a soft but chilly hand
The silken leaves of flowers expand;
Thy tear--set eye shall I ne'er see
Weep o'er a sickly plant like me?
Thou art the nurse of infant flowers,
The parent of relenting showers;
Thy tears and smiles when newly born
Hang on the cheek of weeping Morn,
While Evening sighs in seeming grief
O'er frost--nipp'd bud or bursting leaf.
Once Pity held thee in her arms,

And, breathing all her gentle charms,
Bade thy meek smile o'ertake the tear,
And Hope break loose from trembling Fear;
Bade clouds that load the breast of Day
On melting Twilight weep away;
She bade thee, when the breezy Morn
Kiss'd the sweet gem that deck'd the thorn,
O'er the pale primrose softly pour
The nectar of a balmy shower;
And is the primrose dear to thee?
And wilt thou not give health to me?
See how I droop! my strength decays,
And life wears out a thousand ways;
Supporting friends their cordials give,
And wish, and hope, and bid me live;
With this short breath it may not be,
Unless thou lend'st a sigh to me.
O! fan me with a gentler breeze;
Invite me forth with busy bees;
And bid me trip the dewy lawn
Adorn'd with wild flowers newly blown;
O! do not sternly bid me try
The influence of a milder sky;
I know that May can weave her bower,
And spot, and paint, a richer flower;
Nor is her cheek so wan as thine;
Nor is her hand so cold as mine;
Nor bears she thy unconstant mind,
But ah! to me she ne'er was kind.
To thee I'll rear a mossy throne,
And bring the violet yet unblown;
Then teach it just to ope its eye,
And on thy bosom fondly die;
Embalm it in thy tears, and see
If thou hast one more left for me.
In thy pale noon no roses blow,
Nor lilies spread their summer snow;
Nor would I wish this time--worn cheek
In all the blush of health to break;
No; give me ease and cheerful hours,
And take away thy fairer flowers;
So may the rude gales cease to blow,
And every breeze yet milder grow,
Till I in slumber softly sleep,
Or wake but to grow calm and weep;
And o'er thy flowers in pity bend,
Like the soft sorrows of a friend.

Endorsement To The Deed Of Separation In The April Of 1816 by Lord George Gordon Byron
A year ago, you swore, fond she!

'To love, to honour,' and so forth:
Such was the vow you pledged to me,
And here's exactly what 'tis worth.

Stanzas April 1814 by Percy Bysshe Shelley
Away! the moor is dark beneath the moon,
Rapid clouds have drank the last pale beam of even:
Away! the gathering winds will call the darkness soon,
And profoundest midnight shroud the serene lights of heaven.

Pause not! The time is past! Every voice cries, Away!
Tempt not with one last tear thy friend's ungentle mood:
Thy lover's eye, so glazed and cold, dares not entreat thy stay:
Duty and dereliction guide thee back to solitude.

Away, away! to thy sad and silent home;
Pour bitter tears on its desolated hearth;
Watch the dim shades as like ghosts they go and come,
And complicate strange webs of melancholy mirth.

The leaves of wasted autumn woods shall float around thine head:
The blooms of dewy spring shall gleam beneath thy feet:
But thy soul or this world must fade in the frost that binds the dead,
Ere midnight's frown and morning's smile, ere thou and peace may meet.

The cloud shadows of midnight possess their own repose,
For the weary winds are silent, or the moon is in the deep:
Some respite to its turbulence unresting ocean knows;
Whatever moves, or toils, or grieves, hath its appointed sleep.

Thou in the grave shalt rest—yet till the phantoms flee
Which that house and heath and garden made dear to thee erewhile,
Thy remembrance, and repentance, and deep musings are not free
From the music of two voices and the light of one sweet smile.

A Letter To Dafnis April: 2d 1685 by Anne Kingsmill Finch
This to the Crown, and blessing of my life,
The much lov'd husband, of a happy wife.
To him, whose constant passion found the art
To win a stubborn, and ungratefull heart;
And to the World, by tend'rest proof discovers
They err, who say that husbands can't be lovers.
With such return of passion, as is due,
Daphnis I love, Daphnis my thoughts persue,
Daphnis, my hopes, my joys, are bounded all in you:
Ev'n I, for Daphnis, and my promise sake,
What I in women censure, undertake.
But this from love, not vanity, proceeds;
You know who writes; and I who 'tis that reads.

Judge not my passion, by my want of skill,
Many love well, though they express itt ill;
And I your censure cou'd with pleasure bear,
Wou'd you but soon return, and speak itt here.

On A Nightingale In April by William Sharp
The yellow moon is a dancing phantom
Down secret ways of the flowing shade;
And the waveless stream has a murmuring whisper
Where the alders wave.

Not a breath, not a sigh, save the slow stream's whisper:
Only the moon is a dancing blade
That leads a host of the Crescent warriors
To a phantom raid.
Out of the Lands of Faerie a summons,
A long, strange cry that thrills through the glade: -
The gray-green glooms of the elm are stirring,
Newly afraid.

Last heard, white music, under the olives
Where once Theocritus sang and played -
Thy Thracian song is the old new wonder,
O moon-white maid!

April by Alice Cary
 The wild and windy March once more
Has shut his gates of sleet,
And given us back the April-time,
So fickle and so sweet.

Now blighting with our fears, our hopes -
Now kindling hopes with fears -
Now softly weeping through her smiles -
Now smiling through her tears.

Ah, month that comes with rainbows crowned,
And golden shadows dressed -
Constant to her inconstancy,
And faithful to unrest.

The swallows 'round the homestead eaves -
The bluebirds in the bowers
Twitter their sweet songs for thy sake,
Gay mother of the flowers.

The brooks that moaned but yesterday
Through bunches of dead grass,
Climb up their banks with dimpled hands,
And watch to see thee pass.

The willow, for thy grace's sake,
Has dressed with tender spray,
And all the rivers send their mists
To meet thee on the way.

The morning sets her rosy clouds
Like hedges in the sky,
And o'er and o'er their dear old tunes
The winds of evening try.

Before another week has gone,
Each bush, and shrub, and tree,
Will be as full of buds and leaves
As ever it can be.

I welcome thee with all my heart,
Glad herald of the spring,
And yet I cannot choose but think
Of all thou dost not bring.

The violet opes her eyes beneath
The dew-fall and the rain -
But, oh, the tender drooping lids
That open not again!

Thou set'st the red familiar rose
Beside the household door,
But oh, the friends, the sweet, sweet friends
Thou bringest back no more!

But shall I mourn that thou no more
A short-lived joy can bring,
Since death has lifted up the gates
Of their eternal spring?

Spinning In April by Josephine Preston Peabody
Moon in heaven's garden, among the clouds that wander,
Crescent moon so young to see, above the April ways,
Whiten, bloom not yet, not yet, within the twilight yonder;
All my spinning is not done, for all the loitering days.

Oh, my heart has two wild wings that ever would be flying!
Oh, my heart's a meadow-lark that ever would be free!
Well it is that I must spin until the light is dying;
Well it is the little wheel must turn all day for me!

All the hill-tops beckon, and beyond the western meadows
Something calls for ever, calls me ever, low and clear:
A little tree as young as I, the coming summer shadows,—

The voice of running waters that I always thirst to hear.

Oftentime the plea of it has set my wings a-beating;
Oftentime it coaxes, as I sit weary-wise,
Till the wild life hastens out to wild things all entreating,
And leaves me at the spinning-wheel with dark, unseeing eyes.

San Francisco: April 18,1906 by Ina D Coolbirth
In olden days, a child, I trod thy Sands,
Thy sands unbuilded, rank with brush and briar
And blossom - chased the sea-foam on thy strands,
Young City of my love and my desire.

I saw thy barren hills against the skies,
I saw them topped with minaret and spire;
Wall upon wall thy myriad mansions rise,
Fair City of my love and desire.

With thee the Orient touched heart and hands,
The world-wide argosies lay at thy feet;
Queen of the queenliest land of all the lands -
Our sunset glory, regal, glad and sweet!

I saw thee in thine anguish tortured! prone!
Rent with the earth-throes, garmented in fire!
Each wound upon thy breast upon my own,
Sad City of my grief and my desire.

Gray wind-blown ashes, broken, toppling wall
And ruined hearth—are these thy funeral pyre?
Black desolation covering as a pall—
Is this the end—my love and my desire?

Nay! Strong, undaunted, thoughtless of despaire,
The will that builded thee shall build again,
And all thy broken promise spring more fair,
Thou mighty mother of as mighty men.

Thou wilt arise, invincible! supreme!
The world to voice thy glory never tire;
And song, unborn, shall chant no nobler theme
Great City of my faith and my desire.
But I will see thee ever as of old!
Thy wraith of pearl, wall, minaret and spire,
Framed in the mists that veil thy Gate of Gold
Lost City of my love and my desire.

Here By The Brimming April Streams by Phillip Henry Savage
Here by the brimming April streams,

Here is the valley of my dreams.

Every garden place is seen
Starting up in flames of green;

Breaking forth in yellow gold
Through the blanket of the mold.

Slow unfolded, one by one,
Lantern leaves hang in the sun,

Like the butterflies of June
Weak and wet from the cocoon.

Hastings In April by Bessie Rayner Parkes
IN this rejoicing time, when sun and shower
In shining alternation rule the sky,
And the brown fields are shadow'd every hour
By cloudy masses scudding swiftly by;
Fields soon to smile in greenness, when the breeze
Leaves on the placid water tracks of light,
Or, hurrying, dimples all the crystal seas
With flecking foam and little wavelets bright,--

Then every flower sings out its joyous song;
The wood-anemones, and violets after,
Springing in every Sussex hedge and shaw,
Make all beholders glad with April laughter.
The primrose opens all her folded buds
In yellow beauty to the wooing sun;
Beneath, thro' banks her lavish bounty studs,
The fretting streams o'er stones and branches run.

The celandine, and lilac lady's smock,
Warning the gatherer of the cuckoo near;
The white oxalis, and each old grey rock,
Whence glossy ferns hang down, to artists dear,
In every graceful group; the knotted stumps
Embroider'd with green ivy, the bare down,
With windclipp'd oaks securely set in clumps,
Meet our glad eyes, emerging from the town.

At every step we take the cattle stare
With great soft eyes, which ask when summer's coming,
And days of grateful heat and tranquil air,
Wherein their lazy worships bask till gloaming.
Fast run the little dogs, and snuff the earth,
Or chase the flying birds with vain endeavour;
The cat considers if to venture forth
And greet on sunny flags the warmer weather.

Round go the windmill-sails, and children swarm
At various games; the sick come slowly walking,
Releas'd by this spring day, and you and I
Will pace the High Street for an hour's grave talking--
I mean that rais'd and sunny pavement, high
Above the road, and bounded by a wall
Which dear green trees o'erhang, quite undisturb'd,
Save where our meditative shadows fall,--

Or out into the country, to that bank
Of blue-bell and red orchis, you with drawing,
And I with Tennyson; no creature near
But the quiet donkey peacefully hee-hawing
Over the hedge. So much for Hastings' treasures
Of sight or sound in April. Every time
Of the long year hath others, beautiful,
Gladdening the heart, and meet for duteous rhyme.

Love Like An April Day Beguiles by James Bland Burges
Love like an April day beguiles,
Each moment brings new changes;
From cold to heat, from frowns to smiles,
Capriciously he ranges.
Now he allures to mirth and joy,
And points to scenes of pleasure;
But, ere we reach them, the false boy
Bears off the promis'd treasure.

April by John Bannister Tabb
'How is it you are laughing, dear,
With both your eyes a-twinkle?
Alas, 'tis all too soon, I fear
To let my little buds appear.
But now each restless prisoner
Attempts my foot to tickle,
And once to laugh if I begin,
They know I cannot keep them in.'

April Showers by Menella Bute Smedley
He said there was on earth no fairer sight
Than April shadows from the tall green flags
We taunted him with overflows of light
From walls of sunrise upon Alpine crags;
Or pageantries of tropic flowers that swoon
In the vague, passionate atmosphere of noon;
Or ranks of crested tumult in the deep,
Or banners of broad tempest on the sky,

But he went murmuring, like a man asleep,
About those April shadows constantly,
And once I thought I heard him call them "grand."
I smiled, but scoffed not. Then he took my hand,
And, looking at me gravely, like a man
About to tell a secret, thus began:
The great flags grow sedately. Down in glades
The riot and hurry of the rising spring
Know them for rulers. All their emerald blades,
Threaded with fires of gold, stand near the shades,
Kept trimly ready for some fairy king;
A blossom hides in every guardian sheaf
Till summer calls it. Each particular leaf,
Sharp as a spear and tender as a plume,
Lets fall its little breadth of crystal gloom
To wave and flutter on the windy grass,
Or to lie still, if not a sigh should pass
The lips of patient evening. None can name
The colour of these shadows, for they keep
The tiny snow-stars and the cups of flame
Safe in their shelter, softened, yet the same,
Like sights we love remembered in our sleep.
On the fine limit of their lines of night,
Grasses are gems, and lingering dewdrops sparks;
They are not shadows, they are ambushed Light,
They are not lights, but they are lustrous darks,
Films which no force can rend, no skill hath wrought,
Impalpable and permanent as thought.
I saw them first—and here he dropped his voice,
As if he feared to wrong a sight so choice
By talking of it rashly—on a day
Of long delight, just at the brink of May;
All through rich silence of the woods I heard
The young world growing. Aimless and at ease,
Moving or pausing, like a joyful bird
Who dips and poises on the swinging seas,
For ten delicious hours, at last I found
These shadows making wonderful the ground
For none to see. A sentinel I stood
And watched. No louder footstep than a fay's
Touched the frail echoes, till with long delays
A slow, soft sunset filled and flushed the wood,
And sank and left us.
Then I understood
How all the sweetness of this day of days
Had passed into the shadows, till they wore
(Like that enchanted ring which seals for good
The long love-volume after and before)
Its glory in their heart for evermore.

An April Gust by Elizabeth Stuart Phelps Ward

It shall be as it hath been.
All the world is glad and green-
Hush! Ah, hush! There cannot be
April now for you and me.

Put your finger on the lips
Of your soul; the wild rain drips;
The wind goes diving down the sea;
Tell the wind, but tell not me.

Yet if I had aught to tell,
High as heaven, or deep as hell,
Bent the fates awry or fit,
I would find a word for it.
Oh, words that neither sea nor land
Can lift their ears to understand!
Wild words, as dumb as death or fear,
I dare to die, but not to hear!

Stanzas To April And Invitation To Garibaldi by Janet Hamilton

April's genial sun is shining,
Vernal clouds with 'silver lining,'
Rich and balmy dews distilling,
Flora's opening flower-cups filling
With the pearly treasure;

On her robe of freshest green,
Thousand flow'ry gems are seen
Peeping through the tender grass;
By woodland path and mountain pass
Now we stray with pleasure.

Sweet the tender, tuneful notes
Poured from thousand warbling throats;
Sweet the tale of truth and love,
Softly told by cushat-dove
In his amorous cooing.

Sweet the music of the streams,
Where the poet strays and dreams-
Where the incense he receives,
Of bursting buds and tender leaves,
While the Muses wooing.

Now, sweet Spring, my song must fail;
Other sounds and sights assail-
Sounds of cheers that swelling rise
In one vast pæan to the skies
'Tis the welcome given

To Italia's liberator,
Lion king in heart and feature;
Sight more stirring, more sublime,
Never graced the 'march of time;'
Bless, oh bless him, heaven!

Freedom holds high jubilee
In our land, the brave and free;
Freedom's sons, we greet thee well,
Thy glorious name our cheers shall tell-
'Tis Freedom's incarnation.

See, in that stupendous mass,
Britain's sons united pass,
Waiving claims of rank and birth,
Brethren of one blood on earth,
In this sublime ovation.

Garibaldi, Scotia stands
On tip-toe with extended hands,
Glowing heart, and welcome high,
On the wings of April fly
The land of Wallace calls.

Queen of the West, fair Glasgow's name,
Not last not least in civic fame,
Not last not least upon thy roll
Of friends-she now with heart and soul
Invites thee to her halls.

The Soul Of April by Bliss William Carman
OVER the wintry threshold
Who comes with joy to-day,
So frail, yet so enduring,
To triumph o'er dismay?
Ah, quick her tears are springing,
And quickly they are dried,
For sorrow walks before her,
But gladness walks beside.
She comes with gusts of laughter,—
The music as of rills;
With tenderness-and sweetness, —
The wisdom of the hills.
Her hands are strong to comfort,
Her heart is quick to heed.
She knows the signs of sadness,
She knows the voice of need.
There is no living creature,
However poor or small,
But she will know its trouble,

And hasten to its call.
Oh, well they fare forever,
By mighty dreams possessed,
Whose hearts have lain a moment
On that eternal breast.

Under The April Moon by Bliss William Carman
OH, well the world is dreaming
Under the April moon,
Her soul in love with beauty,
Her senses all a-swoon!
Pure hangs the silver crescent
Above the twilight wood,
And pure the silver music
Wakes from the marshy flood.
O Earth, with all thy transport,
How comes it life should seem
A shadow in the moonlight,
A murmur in a dream?

April Evening, France, April 1916 by John William Streets
O sweet blue eve that seems so loath to die,
Trailing the sunset glory into night,
Within the soft, cool strangeness of thy light,
My heart doth seem to find its sanctuary.

The day doth verge with all its secret care,
The thrush is lilting vespers on the thorn;
In Nature's inner heart seems to be born
A sweet serenity; and over there

Within the shadows of the stealing Night,
Beneath the benison of all her stars
Men, stirr'd to passion by relentless Mars,
Laughing at Death, wage an unceasing fight.

The thunder of the guns, the scream of shells
Now seem to rend the placid evening air:
Yet as the night is lit by many a flare
The thrush his love in one wild lyric tells.

O sweet blue eve! Lingering awhile with thee,
Before the earth with thy sweet dews are wet,
My heart all but thy beauty shall forget
And find itself in thy serenity.

Sonnet To April by Henry Kirke White
Emblem of life! see changeful April sail

In varying vest along the shadowy skies,
Now bidding summer's softest zephyrs rise,
Anon recalling winter's stormy gale,
And pouring from the cloud her sudden hail;
Then, smiling through the tear that dims her eyes,
While Iris with her braid the welkin dyes,
Promise of sunshine, not so prone to fail.
So, to us, sojourners in life's low vale,
The smiles of fortune flatter to deceive,
While still the fates the web of misery weave.
So Hope exultant spreads her a?ry sail,
And from the present gloom the soul conveys
To distant summers and far happier days.

April – And Dying by Anne Reeve Aldrich
Green blood fresh pulsing through the trees,
Blacks buds, that sun and shower distend;
All other things begin anew,
But I must end.

Warm sunlight on faint-colored sward,
Warm fragrance in the breezes' breath;
For other things art heat and life,
For me is death.

Written April 18th 1796 by Matilda Betham
THE beauteous queen of social love,
Descending from the realms above,
Through the wide space of ether flew,
With care this little world to view,
Till, tir'd with wandering, at the last,
Through every different climate past,
She sought not out a splendid dome,
But made this humble cot her home.
The sweetest lyre would strive in vain,
To sing the pleasures of her reign,

Whose powerful influence does impart,
New softness to the feeling heart,
Bids it each narrow thought resign,
And fills it with a warmth benign.
From morning till the close of day,
Here all a grateful homage pay,
For here she plays her harmless wiles,
And scatters her endearing smiles;
Here no proud rivals intervene,
And all, though glowing, is serene.

Here, since she first her visit paid,

Still has the sweet enchantress staid,
And never met a single slight,
Or spread her snowy plumes for flight.
Contented 'neath the humble roof,
No timid heart is kept aloof;
A kind and condescending guest,
She lightens each despairing breast;
Where pain her poignant venom spreads,
The balm of tenderness she sheds,
Which breathes a calm repose around,
And heals at last the burning wound.

When the heart throbs with bitter woe,
Her winning mien disarms the foe,
And the kind glances of her eye,
Force the desponding power to fly.
She gives a zest to every joy,
Forbids tranquillity to cloy,
Softens misfortune, chases fear,
And balm distills in every tear.
'Tis she alone can make us know,
A truly blissful hour below,
Can smooth the furrow'd brow of life,
And hush the thundering voice of strife.

O, may she still exert her power,
Still lead us to the rural bower,
Which vaunting Pride does ne'er disgrace,
Or critic Envy's spiteful face.
Here Raymond ever shall delight,
To sit and watch the closing night;
And open-hearted Gertrude here,
With her sweet infant shall appear.
Here oft her brother shall prepare,
A wreath for Mary's curling hair;
While soft-voic'd Anna, fond of play,
And all the train, alert and gay,

In healthful games shall frolic round,
And revel on the mossy ground.
Here Edmund shall forget his care,
And often fill an elbow chair;
While Sophia, friendly and sincere,
Shall ever find a welcome here.
Yet would my hovering fancy trace,
The features of each happy face;
And sympathy informs my mind,
That they the same emotions find;
That in each scene of harmless glee,
Memory recalls the absent three:
And all, though distance strives to part,

Will hold communication in the heart.

Written On The Day Of General Thanksgiving April 14th 1833 by Henry Alford
Surely, methinks, this Sabbath morn
Some brighter sunshine should adorn
Than Heaven vouchsafes on common days;
And buds should burst, and all the throng
Of busy warblers crowd their song
To help the race of man to praise.

But on its birth no sun hath shined;
Ever the deep voice of the wind
Sweepeth the tree--tops far and near:
And on the branches not a bird
As on past morning--tides, is heard,
But all is winter--bound and drear.

Yet this ungladsome sky may teach
A lesson, and these winds may preach
A sermon in the nation's ear;
And souls not all unapt to learn
Some dim forebodings may discern
Of new disquietude and fear.

Great God, with trembling we rejoice;
The echo of thy warning voice
Yet vibrates in the middle air:
Not yet thy glittering sword of death
Is peaceful laid within its sheath,
Ready to strike, as now to spare.

An April Fool by Alfred Austin
I sallied afield when the bud first swells,
And the sun first slanteth hotly,
And I came on a yokel in cap and bells,
And a suit of saffron motley.

He was squat on a bank where a self-taught stream,
Fingering flint and pebble,
Was playing in tune to the yaffel's scream,
And the shake of the throstle's treble.

``Now, who may you be?'' I asked, ``and where
Do you look for your meals and pillow?''
``My roof,'' he said, ``is the spacious air,
And my curtain the waving willow.
``My meal is a shive of the miller's loaf,
And hunger the grace that blesses:
'Tis banquet enough for a village oaf,

With a handful of fresh green cresses.

"A plague on your feasts where the dish goes round,
Though I know where the truffles burrow,
And the plover's eggs may, in fours, be found,
In the folds of the pleated furrow.

"And my name? O, I am an April Fool,
So yclept in the hamlet yonder;
For when old and young are at work or school,
I sit on a stile and ponder.

"I gather the yellow weasel-snout,
As I wander the woods at random,
Or I stoop stone-still, and tickle the trout,
And at times, for a lark, I land 'em.

"But I flick them back ere they gape and pant,
After gazing at gill and speckle.
For why should I keep what I do not want,
Who can fish without hook or heckle?

"Yes, I am an April Fool: confessed!
And my pate grows not wise for scratching;
But I know where the kingfisher drills his nest,
And the long-tailed tits are hatching."

Then he leaped to his feet, and he shook his bells,
And they jangled all together,
As blithe as the chime that sinks and swells
For the joy of a nuptial tether.

And, as they chimed, in the covert near
Where ripens the juicy whortle,
The rustling whisper reached my ear
Of a loitering maiden's kirtle.

Whereat he laughed: "I'm an April Fool,
But am jocund withal and jolly,
So long as I have this realm to rule,
And a lass to love my folly.

"Go and woo, where the deftly fair parade,
The smiles of a fine court lady;
But I will cuddle my rustic maid,
In the pheasant-drives husht and shady.

"Her cheek is as creamy as milk in June,
And the winds nor chap nor warp it;
We dance, with the blackbird to give the tune,
And with primroses for carpet.

``Her quick-flashing fingers knit the hose
For her little feet neat and nimble;
Her kiss is as sweet as a half-shut rose,
And her laugh like a silver cymbal.

``She never asks how my fortunes fare,
Nor wonders how full my purse is;
She sits on my knee, and she strokes my hair,
And I tell her my wildwood verses.

``She has not a gem she can call her own,
But I rest on a sheepfold hurdle,
And, out of the daffodils newly blown,
Entwine her a golden girdle.

``And soon I shall have for my nut-sweet girl,
When the May tree is adorning
Its weather-tanned skin with rows of pearl,
A new necklace, night and morning.

``When shortly we catch the cuckoo's call,
We shall clap our hands to hear him;
For let whom they may his gibes appal,
This April Fool don't fear him.''

Then a wind-cloud, hued like a ringdove's neck,
Made the rain run helter-skelter;
The keen drops pattered on bank and beck,
And I crouched in the ditch for shelter.

But he whistled his love, and he waved his cap,
And the bells all rang together;
``Just fancy!'' he cried, ``to care one rap
For the whims of wind or weather.

``Through all the seasons I keep my youth,
Which is more than you town-folk do, sir.
Now, which is the April Fool, in sooth?
Do you think it is I,-or you, sir?''

Then the rain ceased slashing on branch and pool,
And swift came the sunshine, after;
And the thrush and the yaffel screamed, ``April Fool!''
And the covert rang with laughter.

Be Ye In Love With April Tide by Clinton Scollard
BE ye in love with April-tide?
I' faith, in love am I!
For now 't is sun, and now 't is shower,

And now 't is frost, and now 't is flower,
And now 't is Laura laughing-eyed,
And now 't is Laura shy.

Ye doubtful days, O slower glide!
Still smile and frown, O sky!
Some beauty unforeseen I trace
In every change of Laura's face:
Be ye in love with April-tide?
I' faith, in love am I!

April 1844 by Henry Alford
There was a child, bright as the summer prime,
Fair as a flower. Not long his speaking eyes
Had uttered meaning: nature's love not long
Had stolen into his heart. One sweet May morn
His young life dawned: so that the Summer heats
Unconscious passed he through; the Autumn fruits
Just gladdened him with bloom; the sparkling frost
Awoke his greeting smile: but when the Spring
Broke out upon the earth, lighting with stars
Of floral radiance all the level green,
Then was his joy a living laughing thing;
He held the coloured buds; their beauty fed
His eager longing; up to those he loved
He held them in the fulness of his joy,
And laughter, eloquent of inward bliss.

Dear child,--for thou wert ours,--this and the like,
A few sweet visions of thine infant smiles,
A few bright hours of purity and calm,
Are all of thee that we remember now:
For in the sunshine of that rising Spring,
When lavish bloom was poured on all around,
Thy cheek alone grew pale: day after day
Thou fadest from our sight: yet even thus,
Long as thine eyes could gaze, thy fingers clasp,
Brought we our tribute due of gleaming buds,
Glad, if we might one moment wake anew
Thy dormant thought, and light thine eyes with joy.

Sonnet LX. Wymeswold, April 1837 by Henry Alford
Dear streamlet, tripping down thy devious course,
Or lulled in smoothest pools of sombre hue,
Or breaking over stones with murmurs hoarse,
To thee one grateful strain is surely due
From me, the poet of thy native wolds,
Now that the sky is golden in the west,
And distant flocks are bleating from their folds,

And the pale eve--star lifts her sparkling crest.
Would it were thus with thee, when summer suns
Shed their strong heats, and over field and hill
Swims the faint air, and all the cattle shuns
The brighter slopes; but then thy scanty rill
Has dwindled to a thread, and, creeping through
The tangled herbage, shelters from the view.

The Famous Speech-Maker Of England Or Baron (Alias Barren) Lovel's Charge At The Assizes At Exon, April 5, 1710 by Jonathan Swift

From London to Exon,
By special direction,
Came down the world's wonder,
Sir Salathiel Blunder,
With a quoif on his head
As heavy as lead;
And thus opened and said:
Gentlemen of the Grand Inquest,

Her majesty, mark it,
Appointed this circuit
For me and my brother,
Before any other;
To execute laws,
As you may suppose,
Upon such as offenders have been.
So then, not to scatter
More words on the matter,
We're beginning just now to begin.
But hold—first and foremost, I must enter a clause,
As touching and concerning our excellent laws;
Which here I aver,
Are better by far
Than them all put together abroad and beyond sea;
For I ne'er read the like, nor e'er shall, I fancy
The laws of our land
Don't abet, but withstand,
Inquisition and thrall,
And whatever may gall,
And fire withal;
And sword that devours
Wherever it scowers:
They preserve liberty and property, for which men pull and haul so,
And they are made for the support of good government also.
Her majesty, knowing
The best way of going
To work for the weal of the nation,
Builds on that rock,
Which all storms will mock,
Since Religion is made the foundation.

And, I tell you to boot, she
Resolves resolutely,
No promotion to give
To the best man alive,
In church or in state,
(I'm an instance of that,)
But only to such of a good reputation
For temper, morality, and moderation.
Fire! fire! a wild-fire,
Which greatly disturbs the queen's peace
Lies running about;
And if you don't put it out,
(That's positive) will increase:
And any may spy,
With half of an eye,
That it comes from our priests and Papistical fry.
Ye have one of these fellows,
With fiery bellows,
Come hither to blow and to puff here;
Who having been toss'd
From pillar to post,
At last vents his rascally stuff here:
Which to such as are honest must sound very oddly,
When they ought to preach nothing but what's very godly;
As here from this place we charge you to do,
As ye'll answer to man, besides ye know who.
Ye have a Diocesan,
But I don't know the man;
The man's a good liver,
They tell me, however,
And fiery never!
Now, ye under-pullers,
That wear such black colours,
How well would it look,
If his measures ye took,
Thus for head and for rump
Together to jump;
For there's none deserve places,
I speak't to their faces,
But men of such graces,
And I hope he will never prefer any asses;
Especially when I'm so confident on't,
For reasons of state, that her majesty won't
Know, I myself I
Was present and by,
At the great trial, where there was a great company,
Of a turbulent preacher, who, cursedly hot,
Turn'd the fifth of November, even the gun-powder plot,
Into impudent railing, and the devil knows what:
Exclaiming like fury—it was at Paul's, London—
How church was in danger, and like to be undone,

And so gave the lie to gracious Queen Anne;
And, which is far worse, to our parliament-men:
And then printed a book,
Into which men did look:
True, he made a good text;
But what follow'd next
Was nought but a dunghill of sordid abuses,
Instead of sound doctrine, with proofs to't, and uses.
It was high time of day
That such inflammation
should be extinguish'd without more delay:
But there was no engine could possibly do't,
Till the commons play'd theirs, and so quite put it out.
So the man was tried for't,
Before highest court:
Now it's plain to be seen,
It's his principles I mean,
Where they suffer'd this noisy and his lawyers to bellow:
Which over, the blade
A poor punishment had
For that racket he made.
By which ye may know
They thought as I do,
That he is but at best an inconsiderable fellow.
Upon this I find here,
And everywhere,
That the country rides rusty, and is all out of gear:
And for what?
May I not
In opinion vary,
And think the contrary,
But it must create
Unfriendly debate,
And disunion straight;
When no reason in nature
Can be given of the matter,
Any more than for shapes or for different stature?
If you love your dear selves, your religion or queen,
Ye ought in good manners to be peaceable men:
For nothing disgusts her
Like making a bluster:
And your making this riot,
Is what she could cry at,
Since all her concern's for our welfare and quiet.
I would ask any man
Of them all that maintain
Their passive obedience
With such mighty vehemence,
That damn'd doctrine, I trow!
What he means by it, ho',
To trump it up now?

Or to tell me in short,
What need there is for't?
Ye may say, I am hot;
I say I am not;
Only warm, as the subject on which I am got.
There are those alive yet,
If they do not forget,
May remember what mischiefs it did church and state:
Or at least must have heard
The deplorable calamities
It drew upon families,
About sixty years ago and upward.
And now, do ye see,
Whoever they be,
That make such an oration
In our Protestant nation,
As though church was all on a fire,
With whatever cloak
They may cover their talk,
And wheedle the folk,
That the oaths they have took,
As our governors strictly require;
I say they are men—(and I'm a judge, ye all know,)
That would our most excellent laws overthrow;
For the greater part of them to church never go;
Or, what's much the same, it by very great chance is,
If e'er they partake of her wise ordinances.
Their aim is, no doubt,
Were they made to speak out,
To pluck down the queen, that they make all this rout;
And to set up, moreover,
A bastardly brother;
Or at least to prevent the House of Hanover.
Ye gentlemen of the jury,
What means all this fury,
Of which I'm inform'd by good hands, I assure ye;
This insulting of persons by blows and rude speeches,
And breaking of windows, which, you know, maketh breaches?
Ye ought to resent it,
And in duty present it,
For the law is against it;
Not only the actors engaged in this job,
But those that encourage and set on the mob:
The mob, a paw word, and which I ne'er mention,
But must in this place, for the sake of distinction.
I hear that some bailiffs and some justices
Have strove what they could, all this rage to suppress;
And I hope many more
Will exert the like power,
Since none will, depend on't,
Get a jot of preferment.

But men of this kidney, as I told you before.
I'll tell you a story: Once upon a time,
Some hot-headed fellows must needs take a whim,
And so were so weak
(Twas a mighty mistake)
To pull down and abuse
Bawdy-houses and stews;
Who, tried by the laws of the realm for high-treason,
Were hang'd, drawn, and quarter'd for that very reason.
When the time came about
For us all to set out,
We went to take leave of the queen;
Where were great men of worth,
Great heads and so forth,
The greatest that ever were seen:
And she gave us a large
And particular charge;
Good part on't indeed
Is quite out of my head;
But I remember she said,
We should recommend peace and good neighbourhood, wheresoever we came;
and so I do here;
For that every one, not only men and their wives,
Should do all that they can to lead peaceable lives;
And told us withal, that she fully expected
A special account how ye all stood affected;
When we've been at St. James's, you'll hear of the matter.
Again then I charge ye,
Ye men of the clergy,
That ye follow the track all
Of your own Bishop Blackall,
And preach, as ye should,
What's savoury and good;
And together all cling,
As it were, in a string;
Not falling out, quarrelling one with another,
Now we're treating with Monsieur,—that son of his mother.

Then proceeded on the common matters of the law; and concluded:

Once more, and no more, since few words are best,
I charge you all present, by way of request,
If ye honour, as I do,
Our dear royal widow,
Or have any compassion
For church or the nation;
And would live a long while
In continual smile,
And eat roast and boil,
And not be forgotten,
When ye are dead and rotten;

That ye would be quiet, and peaceably dwell,
And never fall out, but p—s all in a quill.

The Idler's Calendar. Twelve Sonnets For The Month. April by Wilfrid Scawen Blunt
TROUT—FISHING

This morning, through my window, half awake,
I felt the south wind blow; and presently,
With a tumultuous thrill and then a shake,
The nightingale broke forth in melody.
I rose in haste, and looked at the grey sky,
And read an omen. From its corner next
A book I drew, blest book, where fly on fly
Are all the letters of its well--thumbed text.

I chose my cast, a march--brown and a dun,
And ran down to the river, chasing hope.
At the first throw a mighty trout was on,
A very Samson, fit to burst a rope,
Yet tamed by one sad hank of yielding hair
And Fate, the fisherman of King and Pope.
Upon the grass he lies, and gasps the air,
Four silver pounds, sublimely f at and fair.

Child's Talk In April by Christina Georgina Rossetti
I wish you were a pleasant wren,
And I your small accepted mate;
How we'd look down on toilsome men!
We'd rise and go to bed at eight
Or it may be not quite so late.

Then you should see the nest I'd build,
The wondrous nest for you and me;
The outside rough perhaps, but filled
With wool and down; ah, you should see
The cosy nest that it would be.

We'd have our change of hope and fear,
Small quarrels, reconcilements sweet:
I'd perch by you to chirp and cheer,
Or hop about on active feet,
And fetch you dainty bits to eat.

We'd be so happy by the day,
So safe and happy through the night,
We both should feel, and I should say,
It's all one season of delight,
And we'll make merry whilst we may,

Perhaps some day there'd be an egg
When spring had blossomed from the snow:
I'd stand triumphant on one leg;
Like chanticleer I'd almost crow
To let our little neighbours know.

Next you should sit and I would sing
Through lengthening days of sunny spring;
Till, if you wearied of the task,
I'd sit; and you should spread your wing
From bough to bough; I'd sit and bask.

Fancy the breaking of the shell,
The chirp, the chickens wet and bare,
The untried proud paternal swell;
And you with housewife-matron air
Enacting choicer bills of fare.

Fancy the embryo coats of down,
The gradual feathers soft and sleek;
Till clothed and strong from tail to crown,
With virgin warblings in their beak,
They too go forth to soar and seek.

So would it last an April through
And early summer fresh with dew,
Then should we part and live as twain:
Love-time would bring me back to you
And build our happy nest again.

Home Thoughts From Abroad by Robert Browning
Oh, to be in England
Now that April's there,
And whoever wakes in England
Sees, some morning, unaware,
That the lowest boughs and the brushwood sheaf
Round the elm-tree bole are in tiny leaf,
While the chaffinch sings on the orchard bough
In England—now!

And after April, when May follows,
And the whitethroat builds, and all the swallows!
Hark, where my blossomed pear-tree in the hedge
Leans to the field and scatters on the clover
Blossoms and dewdrops—at the bent spray's edge—
That's the wise thrush; he sings each song twice over,
Lest you should think he never could recapture
The first fine careless rapture!
And though the fields look rough with hoary dew,
All will be gay when noontide wakes anew

The buttercups, the little children's dower
—Far brighter than this gaudy melon-flower!

www.ingramcontent.com/pod-product-compliance
Lightning Source LLC
Chambersburg PA
CBHW061314040426
42444CB00010B/2638